$INE$$

Google

Google apps

First published in 2011 by Wayland
The paperback edition published in 2012 by Wayland
Copyright © Wayland 2011

Wayland
338 Euston Road
London NW1 3BH

Wayland Australia
Level 17/207 Kent Street
Sydney, NSW 2000

Commissioning editor: Camilla Lloyd
Designer: Emma Randall
Picture researcher: Shelley Noronha

Picture Acknowledgements: The author and publisher would like to thank the following for allowing
their pictures to be reproduced in this publication. Cover and 27: © CJG-Technology/Alamy; throughout
backgroun: RedShineStudio/Istock; 1, 5, 9, 10 (bottom), 11, 15 (right), 16, 17, 21, 22, 23, 24, 25, 26:
Google; 4 Xie Zhengyi/AP/Press Association Images; 7 Mark Blinch/Reuters/Corbis Getty Images; 8, 10 (top)
Getty Images; 12 Karl-Josef Hildenbrand/epa/Corbis: 12; 13 copyright and permission by Ruth Kedar; 14
Bertrand Gardel/Hemis/Corbis; 15 (left) Bloomberg via Getty Images; 18 Sipa Press/Rex Features; 20 Philippe
Wojazer/Reuters/Corbis; 28 89 Studio/Shutterstock; 29 Meawpong 34 05/Shutterstock.
Every attempt has been made to clear copyright for this edition. Should there be any inadvertent
omission please apply to the publisher for rectification.

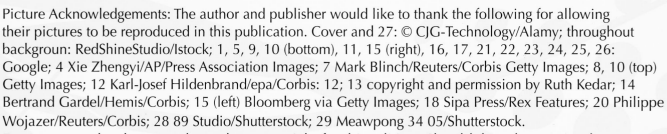

Sutherland, Adam.
    Google. -- (Big business)
    1. Google (Firm)--Juvenile literature. 2. Internet
industry--Juvenile literature.
    I. Title II. Series
    338.7'6102504252-dc22

ISBN: 978 0 7502 7089 2

Printed in China
Wayland is a division of Hachette Children's Books, an Hachette UK company.
www.hachette.co.uk

Contents

The world gets Googled! 4

What makes Google so good? 6

Google is born 8

Setting up the company 10

Standing out from the competition 12

Making a profit 14

Keeping the staff happy 16

Google goes public 18

Expanding the business 20

Diversifying the business 22

Google changes the world 24

Making Google future-proof 26

Invent the next Google product! 28

SWOT analysis 29

Do you have what it takes to work at Google? 30

Glossary 31

Further information 32

Index 32

The world gets Googled!

Google is one of the best-known companies on the planet. Its search engine is used for two-thirds of web searches in the United States, and 70 per cent worldwide. Go to www.Google.co.uk and type something into the search box. Google will examine billions of web pages to find the most relevant pages for your query, and usually brings you the results in less than half a second. No other search engine accesses more of the Internet or delivers more useful information.

A search engine is a website thats purpose is to search for other useful and informative sites when you type something into it. This can be anything and everything from 'Nelson Mandela' to 'cheap flights'. You are then directed quickly and simply to sites that cover your area of interest. Google's skill at delivering useful, targeted search results has been the foundation of their success. But it is only part of the Google story.

What turned the company into the Internet business phenomenon it is today, was realising they could get advertisers to pay for 'sponsored'

▲ *The Google screen in China.*

Larry Page and Sergey Brin have become world famous thanks to Google.

links on every single search they delivered. This financial windfall turned Google into an incredibly successful and powerful company. It took software giant Microsoft 15 years to reach one billion dollars in revenues. It took Google just six!

Like many successful companies, Google does not stand still. It has sought to increase its advertising revenues from search by expanding around the world. At the same time, it has also extended its business model beyond just a search engine. YouTube (see pages 20-21) and Google Maps, Street View and Google Earth (see pages 22-23) are just some of the extra products and services that Google now offers. The Internet company that refined search is now one of the world's biggest brands, and plans to get even bigger.

▼ *The pie chart shows Google's massive dominance of the search market.*

"*The Internet makes information available. Google makes information accessible.*"

Hal Varian, Google's chief economist

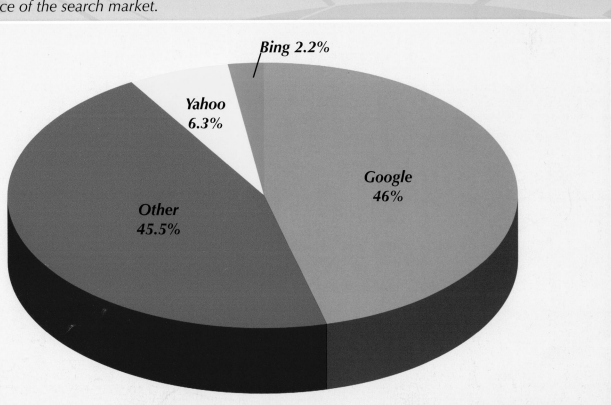

Bing 2.2%

Yahoo
6.3%

Other
45.5%

Google
46%

What makes Google so good?

The key to Google's success is the accuracy and relevance of its search. Their 'secret ingredient' is a mathematical formula that promises to bring you only the most useful links, and even to 'second guess' what your search actually means.

Google places links at the top of your search that have previously generated the most 'traffic' (ie clicks and visits from other people). They also give higher ranking to links from reputable news sources like the BBC or *The Times*. By monitoring how many people click on a link, or how many other websites find it interesting enough to link to, Google decides whether that link is 'relevant' and gives it a value. This value is known as PageRank™, after one of Google's founders, Larry Page.

To make your search as fast as possible, Google has created its own 'copied' version of the Internet. The site has scanned and ranked several billion Web pages – the figure increases daily – and stored them on its own computers, known as 'servers'. The pages are organised by subject and every time you click 'Search' hundreds of thousands of computers get to work collecting different document links and returning those links to your screen in the blink of an eye.

The search is speeded up because Google stores three copies of all its previous searches, so it doesn't have to scan the entire Web if two people ask the same question.

To help make each person's search more relevant to their personal needs, Google relies on software files called 'cookies'. These files live on your computer and keep track of your online activities – what search questions you ask, what websites you visit, how long you spend on each site, what ads you click on, and what you buy online.

Because of these cookies, Google's search gets better the more you use it, as the company becomes familiar with the kind of information you are looking for.

Cookies don't identify you by name and address, but they do provide lots of valuable information on each computer's user that Google can share with advertisers.

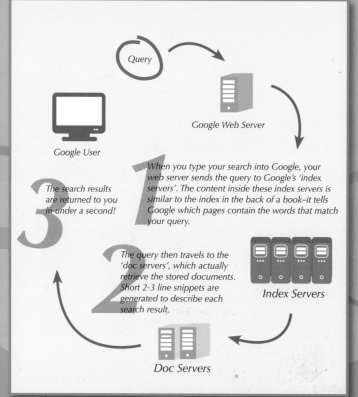

Query

Google Web Server

Google User

The search results are returned to you in under a second!

1 When you type your search into Google, your web server sends the query to Google's 'index servers'. The content inside these index servers is similar to the index in the back of a book–it tells Google which pages contain the words that match your query.

2 The query then travels to the 'doc servers', which actually retrieve the stored documents. Short 2-3 line snippets are generated to describe each search result.

Index Servers

Doc Servers

▼ *The black background was used by Google to support Earth Hour when people were encouraged to turn off their lights for one hour to make a statement about climate change, March 2008.*

Business Matters

The Unique Selling Proposition or Point (USP) — a USP is some unique quality about a company's product or service that will attract customers to use or buy it rather than an alternative product from a competitor. When it first appeared, Google was not the only search engine that people could use, but it stood out from competitors like Excite and Yahoo because of its 'functionality' (what it could do), its appearance (how it looked) and its quality (how it worked).

Google is born

Google founders Larry Page and Sergey Brin met at Stanford University in 1995. The two men had a lot in common. Both were born in 1973, both were obsessed with computers from an early age, and both were studying for PhDs (higher level university degrees) in computer science.

When Larry arrived at Stanford, Sergey had already been there for two years and was part of the team who welcomed Larry to the campus. Apparently the pair disagreed on just about everything during that first meeting, but gradually they got to know each other and became firm friends.

One night, Larry woke up from a dream with his vision for Google fully formed in his head. 'I was thinking: What if we could download the whole Web, and just keep the links... I grabbed a pen and started writing!'

Larry realised that the links between sites – the shortcuts and 'road signs' that told you where to go and why –

▼ *Google co-founders (Sergey left, Larry right) in their messy office in Mountain View, California in 2002.*

were the result of conscious effort. Internet users were 'voting' for the best links whenever they chose to visit a website, or when they included a link on their own site. Larry started downloading the entire structure of the Internet – something that Google is still doing today!

Larry's project also caught Sergey's imagination, and the two men became obsessed not just with creating a new search engine, but with creating the best, most useful, most efficient search engine ever. Their project was first called BackRub (apparently a reference to their mathematical formula, which counts backlinks as 'votes'), but the pair soon changed the name to Google, a common misspelling of 'googol', or 10100 – the amount of traffic that they hoped the website would one day handle.

> " I realised I wanted to invent things, but I also want to change the world. Inventing things isn't enough, you have to get them out into the world and have people use them to have any effect. So probably from when I was 12, I knew I was going to start a company eventually. "
>
> ***Larry Page***

Brains Behind The Brand

Larry Page – Co-Founder and President, Products

Larry Page was Google's founding Chief Executive Officer (CEO) and grew the company to more than 200 employees and increased profitability before moving into his current role as President of Products in April 2001. Larry continues to share responsibility for Google's day-to-day operations with fellow company directors Eric Schmidt and Sergey Brin.

A company president's main responsibilities are to ensure that all lines of business – in Larry's case, the 'products' that Google launches – are running efficiently and within a budget set by the board of directors. The company president usually works with senior-level managers to devise plans that will generate revenues, create new business opportunities, and help the company remain competitive in the marketplace.

◄ *Larry's love of technology began at the age of six, when he became an award-winning junior scientist.*

Setting up the company

Larry and Sergey delivered a 'paper' – an academic study – on Google to their Stanford professors in January 1998. It was called 'The Anatomy of a Large-Scale Hypertextual Web Search Engine', and can still be seen at http://infolab.stanford.edu/~backrub/google.html.

At first, both men wanted to finish their studies, but eventually decided to take a break from Stanford to found Google and try to make a success of it as a company. They reasoned that they would both come back and finish their PhDs if things didn't work out.

In September 1998, Google got its first investment – four investors putting in around $250,000 (£156,000) each. One of the investors was Amazon.com owner Jeff Bezos. Larry and Sergey rented their first office space for $1,700 (£1,000) per month – 232 Santa Margarita Avenue, a double garage and two downstairs spare rooms of a house in Menlo Park, in the Bay Area of California, south of San Francisco. Their office space consisted of three tables, three chairs, a small fridge, an old washing machine, and a table tennis table folded up in the corner because they didn't have the space to play on it.

▲ *This is the first Google headquarters in Santa Margarita Avenue.*

They kept the garage door open for ventilation and their desks were pine doors resting on trestle tables. On the garage door they put a sign saying 'Google Worldwide Headquarters'!

Apart from its initial $1 million (£624,000) investment, Google had a $20,000 (£12,500)

▼ *This is the Google offices in Dublin, Ireland.*

per month contract to provide specialised search results to a consulting company. Nevertheless, Larry and Sergey were determined to move quickly and keep growing. At that stage Google had indexed just 10 per cent of the Web. By the end of 1998, there were six engineers crammed into the garage, so the company relocated to a bigger space above a bike shop in Palo Alto. A second round of funding followed in June 1999, with an investment of $25 million (£15.6 million). That summer, they were up to 40 employees. Google was on its way.

▲ *Sergey has published more than a dozen academic papers on search engines, is a recipient of a National Science Foundation Graduate Fellowship and has been a featured speaker at several international academic, business and technology events.*

Brains Behind The Brand

Sergey Brin – Co-Founder and President, Technology

Sergey was born in Moscow but moved to the USA when he was seven years old. His father was a professor of mathematics at the University of Maryland, and his mother was a scientist at NASA's Goddard Space Flight Centre. After graduating from the University of Maryland, Sergey received a National Science Foundation scholarship to study computer science at Stanford.

Sergey co-founded Google in 1998, and continues to share responsibility for day-to-day operations with fellow directors Larry Page and Eric Schmidt. While Larry focuses on the products, Sergey loves to explore the technology! Among other tasks, Sergey tries to find ways to improve Google Search, making it faster and more accurate than ever.

Business Matters

Forming a company — a 'limited' or 'incorporated' company is a business owned by shareholders (people who own shares in the company), and run by directors. The company's shares have a basic value, for example £1 each, which stays the same, and a 'market value', which goes up and down depending on how good an investment the shares are judged to be by people outside the company who want to buy those shares.

Standing out from the competition

Other search engines like Excite, Lycos and Yahoo were developing into portals (gateways to larger, more sophisticated websites containing general interest content, news and so on), and trying to keep visitors on their sites. Google, however, remained focused on the importance of search, and providing users with the best possible free service, giving them the answer to their questions and directing them away from Google as quickly as possible.

This focus on simplicity can be seen in the Google homepage. The page loads quickly, and the clean design makes it absolutely clear how to proceed in your search for information. Despite many offers from advertisers who wanted banners on the homepage, Larry and Sergey were determined to have a simple, functional front page without advertising or pictures. They also wanted something that looked very different from other search engines.

The pair hired Ruth Kedar to create Google's distinctive multi-coloured logo, which is meant to look, according to Kedar (opposite), 'almost non-designed... The colours evok[ing] memories of child play'.

From 1999 to 2000 the number of searches Google was handling rose from 500,000 per day to 7 million. But Larry and Sergey still didn't know how to make money from Google. Their first plan was to charge companies for delivering valuable information from advanced search results. The pair never wavered, however, from their belief that a great search engine would eventually be a huge success.

Gradually, Google got its foot on the corporate ladder. A deal was signed to make Google the default search engine on Web browser Netscape, which meant a huge boost in traffic.

For a long time, Larry and Sergey avoided the idea of ads on the site, worrying it would slow down the searches. In 2000, their revenues were $19.1 million (£11.9 million), but their losses were $14.7 million (£9.2 million). Google were quickly burning through their cash.

These are the homepages for Yahoo, Google and Bing search engines.

> **"** We deliver the world's information in one click. **"**
>
> *Larry Page*

Artist and designer Ruth Kedar is the person responsible for the distinctive Google logo.

Business Matters

Branding — all the qualities and features of a product, including its name and its appearance, are presented to the customer as a brand. To be successful, all brands — from Google to McDonalds to Nike — need to be distinctive (stand out in some way from competitors), consistent (always provide the same level of quality, and therefore be seen as reliable), recognisable (through a logo or 'look' of a product) and attractive. Everyone recognises Google's simple white homepage and multicoloured logo!

Making a profit

By the end of 2000, Google was the most visited search engine on the Web, with one hundred million daily search queries, and a worldwide market share of 40 per cent. But it was only with the invention of two computer programs – AdWords and AdSense – that it started to become profitable.

AdWords, introduced in October 2000, allows potential advertisers to bid to place small text ads (the ads you see as 'sponsored links' on the right-hand page of a Google search) next to the results for key word searches. British Airways and EasyJet might compete for ad space next to keywords like 'flights' or 'holiday', for example.

All auctions for ads are run online through an automated system. The highest bidder for a keyword gets to place a small text ad that appears at the top of the shaded box to the right of the search results. Up to ten lower bidders also get ad space below the winner.

Google sets the minimum bid per ad word – common words like 'holiday' might cost one or two pence, while more specialised words like 'helicopter parts' might fetch £50 per click.

AdSense is a separate program that brings together web advertisers with websites that want advertising. For example, placing a football boot manufacturer with a sports news website, or a lawyer with a legal advice site. The system is automated and simple – there are no ad sales people, and no bartering over prices.

Google's system – cost per click (CPC) – makes sure that advertisers are only charged when the user clicks on an ad.

▲ Millions of people search Google to get the best holiday deals.

In 2008, Google paid out $5 billion (£3.15 billion) to its hundreds of thousands of ad partners while still making a significant profit. Google could now tap into the lucrative web advertising market and make a profit for the first time. Company profits for 2008 were $4.2 billion (£2.65 billion) on revenues of $21.8 billion (£13.7 billion). Ninety seven per cent of this revenue came from advertising!

Advertisers are provided with an efficient, measurable service. They can count the amount of clicks they receive, and so can decide where they should be spending their money. According to Google, consumers also benefit because they only see adverts that are relevant to them.

> Eric is the leader for the company. Larry and Eric and I all share in the top-level leadership, but mostly Eric takes on the hardest challenges. Larry and I spend more time on products and technology.
>
> **Sergey Brin**

▼ *This is an Adsense page.*

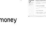

Brains Behind The Brand

Dr Eric Schmidt – Chairman of the Board and Chief Executive Officer (CEO)

Since joining Google in 2001, Eric has helped grow the company from a Silicon Valley start-up to a global enterprise. With founders Sergey Brin and Larry Page, Eric oversees Google's technical and business strategy. Under Eric's leadership, the company's business has extended far beyond search. One of Eric's roles is to remain 'customer focused' – this means he has to make sure that all Google's new 'products' – Earth, Maps, Books etc – are useful and, most importantly, easy to use.

Before joining Google, Eric was the Chairman and CEO of Novell, and Chief Technology Officer at Sun Microsystems, Inc., where he led the development of a famous computer program called Java. ➡

Keeping the staff happy

Google's continued success is partly based on attracting the best and brightest talents in Silicon Valley, and hanging onto them in the face of competition from other big high-tech companies. One way Google fosters worker satisfaction is through its great working conditions.

Google's HQ in Mountain View, California – known as the Googleplex – is like a huge, luxury housing estate. It is a collection of two and three storey buildings with outdoor tables and park benches shaded by trees. There is a vegetable garden, volleyball courts, and bicycles are provided for employees to travel between the buildings.

Members of staff are offered free on-site massages and haircuts, pet care facilities, and three free healthy meals a day from award-winning chefs. Google spends $70 million (£44 million) every year on free meals and snacks for their employees. Also available are carwashes, dry cleaners, vets, gyms, and five doctors' surgeries offering free medical care. Wi-fi equipped buses bring employees to and from work, running from early morning to late at night.

Employees all get a free laptop, and most are also given one day per week (20 per cent of their time) to work on projects they feel passionately about. The policy obviously works. One employee, Google's principal research scientist

The Google office in the Netherlands has its own indoor cycle lane.

Google employees working at the Chicago office.

Krishna Bharat, invented Google News (http://news.google.co.uk/) with his 20 per cent time! Salaries are average, but most employees are offered 'stock options' (shares in Google), meaning that every year, they receive a percentage of the company's profits (known as dividends, see pages 18-19). In 2008, Google paid out a massive $1.1 billon (£690 million) in dividends, often turning members of staff into millionaires overnight!

Not surprisingly, in 2007 and 2008 *Fortune* magazine named Google as the best US company to work for. At the start of 2008, Google employed 20,000 people, and was adding an extra 150 people every week. During the year they received 1,000,000 job applications!

Brains Behind The Brand

Laszlo Bock – Vice President, People Operations

Laszlo is Google's worldwide head of human resources. It is his job to attract talented people to join Google, provide them with the training and development opportunities they need to keep growing, and then stop them being 'head hunted' by other competing hi-tech firms!

Laszlo holds a degree in International Relations from Pomona College, and an MBA from the Yale University School of Management.

Business Matters

Human Resources — the Human Resources (HR) department of a company is responsible for putting in place and maintaining the business practices that allow effective people management. Some key responsibilities of an HR department are: 1) training; 2) staff appraisal: a formal process, performed by managers on their staff, which aims to communicate how they are performing and to discuss what they need in order to improve and develop; 3) staff development: the processes in the company designed to identify the people with potential, keep them in the organisation, and move them into the right positions.

Google goes public

Google was expanding, and hired its first CEO, Eric Schmidt, in February 2001. In 2003 the company passed 500 shareholders and US law stated that within a year they had to offer their shares for sale on the stock market, or open their 'accounts' (the details of their income and costs) to the public.

Larry and Sergey did not want to sell shares in Google as they preferred to keep the running of the company private, but they decided that was a better option than risk competitors gaining valuable information by looking at their accounts. So on August 19, 2004 Google shares went on sale on the New York Stock Exchange in a process called an IPO (which means 'initial public offering').

Investment bankers were hoping for a price of $85 (£55) per share, but trading ended on the first day at $100! The stock reached $108.31 the following day, and by January 31, 2005 had jumped to nearly $200.

In the early days of Google, all new employees were offered stock options (see pages 16-17). This meant they owned part of the company and would make a percentage of the value of the company if and when they ever sold their stock. At the end of the first day's trading more than 900 Google millionaires had been created. Eventually, seven directors – including Larry and Sergey (who owned 32 per cent of the company each) and Eric Schmidt (who owned 6.1 per cent) – would become billionaires.

The Nasdaq Stock Market in New York welcomes Google to the stock market in 2004.

Larry and Sergey were just 31 years old but they remained focused on expanding and growing the business. They stressed to all shareholders that the company would not accept money from advertisers for a better search ranking. What's more, underperforming (and therefore less relevant) ads, would drop down to a lower position on the Google search page, and more relevant ads would move up, even if advertisers had paid less for them! The PageRank™ system – based on usefulness rather than profit – proved that Google was not interested in sacrificing their long-term success or the usefulness of the product for short-term financial gain.

▼ *This graph shows the profit, loss and revenue figures for Google.*

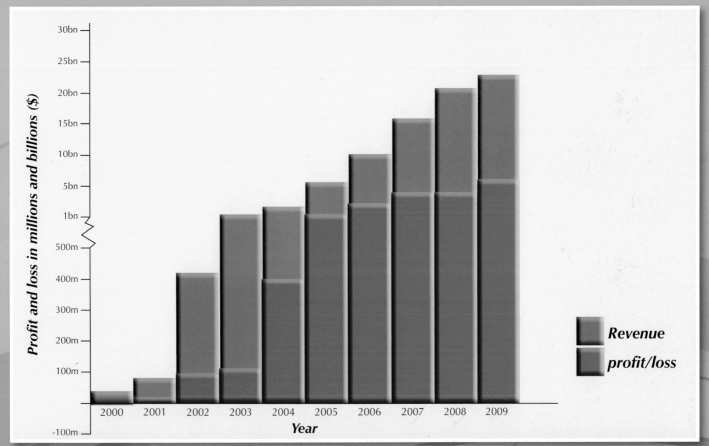

Business Matters

Company shareholders — shareholders at companies like Google hope to make money in two ways. Firstly, as the company makes money, the value of its shares will rise, so an investor can make a profit if he or she sells their shares (known as a 'capital gain'). Secondly, part of the profit that a company makes every year can be given to shareholders based on how many shares they own. This is called a 'dividend'.

In October 2006, Google bought video clips website www.YouTube.com for a massive $1.65 billion (£1 billion). The media world was stunned. YouTube was attracting 34 million monthly views, and four out of every ten video website visitors. But it was making no money!

YouTube founders Chad Hurley and Steve Chen saw Google's offer as a way, not only of allowing them to strengthen the video site's technical infrastructure (which was struggling to cope with the huge number of users), but also to help them work out how to get the site to make money.

Chad and Steve built YouTube as a quick and easy way for them to upload and share video clips with their friends. The site soon became somewhere millions of visitors could watch a large selection of 'user-generated content' (UGC) – home videos, clips of pets, and events recorded with handheld video cameras.

▼ *Chad Hurley and Steve Chen, co-founders of YouTube, attend a news conference in Paris in 2007.*

Business Matters

Market research — all successful companies understand the market in which they are operating, and the actions of their competitors. For Google, this means understanding what the site's users want, and what other search engines are in competition with them. They watch the market closely and take note of any changes. For example, when people started spending more time online through their mobile phones, Google launched a mobile search service.

As time went on, though, users started posting music videos, sports clips and shows like US comedy programme *Saturday Night Live* that they had recorded from television.

Commercial TV channels like ITV1 and Channel 4 attract viewers with programmes produced by other companies, and then sell advertising. Google believed it could make YouTube profitable in the same way. The longer people stayed on the site looking at clips, the more pages they would view, and the more page views, the higher the ad rates would become.

But Google still faces several problems before it can make YouTube profitable. Firstly, the website doesn't own any clips that appear on it, and only avoids being sued by TV and film companies by immediately removing any content it is asked to take down.

Secondly, the TV networks, record companies and film studios are demanding large 'licensing' fees to allow YouTube to keep their content on the site. Google has offered a generous split of ad revenues, but there have been only a limited number of agreements, and as late as 2009 YouTube still lost $500 million (£313 million). Has Google made a costly mistake with YouTube? Only time will tell.

Omid was previously vice president ➤
of business development and sales at Internet pioneer Netscape Communications. He grew online revenue from $88 million (£55 million) to more than $200 million (£125 million) in just 18 months.

Brains Behind The Brand

Omid Kordestani – Senior Advisor, Office of the CEO and Founders
The first non-engineer to be hired by Google, Omid joined the company in 1999 as senior vice president of global sales and business development. He was directly responsible for the company's worldwide revenue generation, as well as the day-to-day management of the sales team. Omid helped bring Google to profitability in record time, generating more than $10 billion (£6.2 billion) in revenue in 2006. Omid is now focused on identifying new revenue opportunities for Google.

Diversifying the business

There's now much more to Google than search. In this spread we focus on some of Google's other 'products'.

Google TV (http://www.google.com/tv/) – allows you to access the Internet, and a wide range of apps through your home television. Search for your favourite shows and Google TV will find all the content available – from TV shows, to web clips to apps – and allow you to access it all with just one click!

Google Earth (http://www.google.com/earth/index.html) – launched in 2005, this 'virtual globe' provides satellite images from around the world, allowing users to zoom into busy London shopping streets or war-torn Baghdad.

Chrome (http://www.google.com/chrome) – Google's web browser, released in 2008, provides easy access to all Google's applications. As of October 2010, it had captured 9.71 per cent of the web browser market, compared to Internet Explorer's 44.72 per cent.

Google Maps (http://maps.google.co.uk/) – launched in 2005, this allows users to plan routes and follow map directions by foot, in the car, or on public transport.

Google Videos (http://video.google.com/) – this free video sharing website and search engine, launched in 2005, has failed to capture a significant share of the online video market, and in 2009 discontinued the ability for users to upload videos.

Google Docs (https://docs.google.com/#all) – launched in 2005, this free, Web-based word processing, presentation and data storage service is extremely popular. It offers 'cloud computing'

▼ *Google Earth provides satellite images of the planet's nearly 60 million square miles.*

Brains Behind The Brand

Susan Wojcicki – Vice President, Product Management

Susan joined Google in 1999 as the company's first marketing manager. She worked on the initial 'viral marketing' programmes to get people talking about and using the search engine. She also led the development of several important products including Google Images, Google Books and Google Video.

Gmail also features instant messaging. ▼

– storing large documents securely on the Internet rather than on your home computer.

Gmail (http://mail.google.com/mail/)– Google's free email service was launched in 2007. Unlike services like Yahoo, which offer 4Mb of storage, Google offers 1 Gigabyte, 250 times as much.

Google Books (http://books.google.com/) – launched in 2004, this aims to digitise and make searchable every book ever published. Google believes the project will bring back to life out-of-print books, but publishing companies and authors argue that it will damage book sales.

Google eBooks (http://books.google.com/ebooks) – like many companies, Google also launched an eBookstore in late 2010.Downloads can be read on computers, Android and Apple devices, but not on Amazon's Kindle.

Google News (http://news.google.com/) – launched in 2002, this offers free access to content from 25,000 publishers worldwide. It is completely non-biased and independent.

Business Matters

Diversification — companies often decide to offer new products or services — like Google Maps and Street View — because it reduces the risk of its other products becoming too limited or uninteresting. By adding new 'products' to its range, Google is providing an extra reason for users to visit the site. When companies offer a completely different product or service, like supermarkets offering car or house insurance, this is called diversification and 'brandstretching'.

Google changes the world

Google has helped change the way we all access information. Larry and Sergey's revolutionary search engine appeared at the start of a decade that saw more and more people going online, and the beginning of a dramatic improvement in high-speed Internet access into homes worldwide. Google Search made 'navigating' the Internet much simpler, and in turn increased the number of people searching for resources online. The Internet generation was born.

And the Internet generation, according to author Chris Anderson, who wrote the recent book *Free: The Future of a Radical Price*, want their information for nothing! So Google, which makes over 90 per cent of its income from advertising, can provide the best free access to information resources around the world – and get advertisers to pay for it.

This business model works the same way for commercial television broadcasters like ITV and Channel 4 in the UK. Their programmes are funded by the money they receive from brands to advertise their products during commercial breaks. But TV channels are now feeling 'the Google effect' – they are losing viewers as more people spend time online, watching video clips

▼ *Google employees hold an informal meeting at the Dublin office.*

on sites like YouTube. Viewing figures are falling, and TV channels are forced to drop their ad rates as a result.

Google's ad system, which allows advertisers to track and monitor every mouse click, is also eating into traditional print advertising. So even though Google Search and Google News are generating more than one billion clicks per month to newspaper websites, newspapers are still in danger of closing down because they can't make money from the Internet traffic.

Google has been a big winner from the Internet generation, but they are also aware that nothing lasts forever. Just as traditional media is being replaced by the Internet, even formerly large Internet companies like Lycos, MySpace and Yahoo have seen their fortunes rise and fall. To maintain their success in ten, 20, even 50 years from now, Google are devoting a lot of time planning for the future.

> " [Larry and I] agree 80-90 per cent of the time. If we both feel the same way, we're probably right... If we both agree and nobody else agrees with us, we assume we're right! That's sort of what you need to do to make progress. "
> **Sergey Brin**

Brains Behind The Brand

Marissa Mayer – Vice President, Search Products & User Experience

Marissa joined Google in 1999 as the company's first female engineer. In the last ten years she has worked on internationalising the Google website into more than 100 languages, refining Google News and Gmail, and launching more than 100 features and products on Google.com.

Marissa now leads the company's product management team on search products – web search, images, news, books, products, maps, Google Earth, Google Toolbar, Google Desktop, Google Health, Google Labs and more.

◄ In 2008, at just 33, Marissa became the youngest woman ever to be included on Fortune magazine's Most Powerful Women list.

Making Google future-proof

Google is also concerned about the environment. This is an overview of the solar panel installation at Googleplex, California.

Where will Google go from here? Right now, it is the undisputed king of search, and it is working hard not to stand still.

To survive and prosper in the long term, Google needs to make itself an essential part of our lives, just as Google Search is within its own market. Already, several of Google's products – particularly the email service Gmail, along with Google Maps, Google Earth, Street View and Google Docs – are extremely successful and widely used, but others like Google Videos have failed to match the competition.

So how does Google plan to stay relevant? One way it can grow is by trying to 'buy success'. Like the purchase of YouTube, it could use its considerable funds to buy into other successful businesses. It was outbid by Microsoft when Facebook sold 1.6 per cent of its shares in October 2007, but there will no doubt be other

purchases that see Google growing into new, unexpected areas.

Like all successful companies, Google is facing competition, most significantly from software giant Microsoft. The huge computer company is heavily promoting its own search engine, Bing, which launched in May 2009 and merged with the established Yahoo brand in July 2009. So far, Bing is a long way behind Google's search numbers (see page 5) but it's trying hard to increase its share of the search market and the advertising revenues that go with it.

Google has always been known for product innovation, and the quality of its search, and it reinforced those qualities with the launch in

Brains Behind The Brand

Vinton G Cerf – Vice President and Chief Internet Evangelist

Widely known as a 'Father of the Web', Vinton was the co-designer with Robert Kahn of the TCP/IP software code that is used to transmit data across the Internet. The invention won both men the highest civilian honour bestowed in the USA, the Presidential Medal of Freedom for 'transform[ing] global commerce, communication and entertainment'.

Vinton holds a PhD in Computer Science from UCLA and more than a dozen honorary degrees. Hugely experienced and respected around the world, Vinton is responsible for identifying new 'enabling technologies' and applications on the Internet and other platforms for Google. In other words, he's looking for technologies that we will be using in five, ten and 20 years' time.

2010 of Google Instant. The new, improved search delivers results before you have even finished typing!

What's more, Google will continue to focus on boosting its revenue from advertising sales, and hope to increase its dominance of the online advertising market. In April 2007 it bought DoubleClick, a company that allows websites like MySpace to sell online ads, and advertisers and ad agencies to buy them. Google plans to be around for many, many years to come.

> " We began as a technology company, and have evolved into a software, technology, internet, advertising and media company all rolled into one. "
>
> **Eric Schmidt, Google CEO**

Google can be accessed directly on iPads and smartphones.

Invent the next Google product!

To create a new product, it is helpful to put together a product development brief like the one below. This is a sample brief for Google TV.

SWOT analysis on the page opposite can help you to think about the strengths, weaknessess, opportunities and threats of your product. This can let you to see how feasible and practical your idea is before you think of investing in it.

Product Development Brief

Name of product: Google TV

Type of product: A searchable archive of TV shows from around the world, sourced from archives like BBCiPlayer, 4OD and so on.

The product explained (use 25 words or less): TV lovers – you never need to leave your computer to watch your favourite programmes from around the world. Any programme at any time!

Target age of users: 1-100

What does the product do? The product allows Google users to access archived TV shows from around the world – from *EastEnders* to *Lost* to *The X-Factor*. Google TV stores every episode of every show with partner TV channels, allowing viewers to catch up on any episodes they have missed. The shows can run with new Google-placed adverts in them to maximise revenue for Google.

What makes your product different? TV viewers who want to catch up on their favourite programmes currently have to visit individual websites – BBC iPlayer, 4OD etc – but this product will put the content from all of these sites into one place, and make them easily searchable and watchable. It will become the 'one-stop shop' for TV addicts around the world!

Name of Google product you are assessing ... Google TV
The table below will help you assess your Google product. By addressing all four areas, you can make your application stronger, and more likely to be a success.

Questions to consider

Does your product do something unique?

Is there anything innovative about it?

Does it have any additional uses?

What are its USPs (unique selling points)?

Strengths

No other similar products currently available.

It's USP is that it brings every television programme in the world onto your computer, and allows you to search them!

Why wouldn't people use this product?

How many channels are currently available to access?

Does it do everything it says it can?

Does it work on all kinds of computers – PCs and Macs?

Weaknesses

People might prefer spending time sitting comfortably in their living rooms watching television.

The product at the moment can only access the programmes that each television broadcaster makes available. This means it is limited.

Will the issue that the product tackles become more important over time?

Will new markets emerge for this product?

Can the product target new 'niche' (ie small, specific) markets?

Can it be used globally?

Can it develop new USPs?

Opportunities

People will become more 'time poor' – in other words, their free time will get less, and therefore more important to them, so this product will become more important.

More and more TV channels will create archives for their TV shows, so the product will have more and more content as time goes on.

Can be used around the world.

Is the market (ie Google traffic) shrinking?
Are people moving to other search engines?

Will new technology make your product unnecessary?

Are any of your weaknesses so bad they might affect the application in the long run?

Will competitors produce a better product?

Threats

Google traffic is still strong and growing, but there will definitely be other search engines trying to compete.

A TV broadcaster like Sky or Virgin in the UK might be able to produce a similar service.

Do you have what it takes to work at Google? Try this!

1) You have a maths homework question you don't understand. Do you:

a) Leave it. You'll ask the teacher tomorrow.

b) Ask your mum, then write down anything, just to get it finished.

c) Go online and research it. You're not going to let one question beat you!

2) You have a presentation to do at school. Do you:

a) Not prepare. You always think better on your feet.

b) Jot down some notes off the top of your head. You'll look at them to remind you.

c) Spend a week preparing handouts for your classmates, and a Powerpoint presentation to show on the pull-down screen in the classroom.

3) You're given a Rubik's Cube as a present. Do you:

a) Leave it in a box under your bed.

b) Have a go at solving it, but get stuck after doing one side.

c) Solve it in half an hour, then start working on designing a better Rubik's Cube with 8 sides instead of 6.

4) It's coming up to your exams. Do you:

a) Not worry about it. You're going to work for your dad anyway.

b) Get all the text books out and read through your work until you get bored.

c) Prepare detailed revision timetables and produce notes on each subject. You want all A*s!

5) You're given a computer for Christmas. Do you:

a) Use it for MSN and watching YouTube

b) Use it for homework, email... MSN and watching YouTube

c) Take out the motherboard and reconfigure it to make it faster and more efficient.

6) Your hero is:

a) Peter Kay – he's the funniest comedian in the country.

b) Nelson Mandela – he fought for what he believed in, and ended Apartheid in South Africa.

c) Nikola Tesla – his work led to the development of electricity, X-rays and wireless communication.

Results

Mostly As: Sorry, but your chance of working at Google is looking shaky! It doesn't sound like you have the interest in computers or logical thinking to succeed at this world-famous company.

Mostly Bs: You are thoughtful and hard-working, but you need to work on standing out from the pack if you want to succeed in a very competitive business.

Mostly Cs: It sounds like you have what it takes to get a job at Google! Keep working hard at school, and pushing to be the best and who knows?

app   short for application. An app is computer software that helps the user perform a task.

barter   to negotiate or haggle over the price of something.

Chief Internet Evangelist   Google's own made-up term for Vinton Cerf.
An evangelist is someone who preaches or spreads the word, usually of God, in order to make people into believers. In Vinton's case, he spreads the word on the Internet to make people believe in its potential.

corporate   relating to the structure and organisation of a company.

digitise   to turn a physical product, like a book, into a digital version that can be read on computers.

discontinue   to stop producing something.

distinctive   recognisable; eye-catching.

diversify   to vary products and services in order to expand or to spread risk.

efficient   working in the most effective way with the least waste of time or resources.

enterprise   another word for a company.

foster   to promote or encourage.

founding a company   to start or launch a company.

functional   practical; working efficiently without fuss.

graduate   to receive a university degree.

infrastructure   the basic structure of a company; how it is organised into departments.

lucrative   profitable.

market share   the percentage of a market that a company controls.

obsessed   focussed completely on something or someone.

PC   short for personal computer.

phenomenon   remarkable or outstanding.

portal   an entrance or gateway (in this case, to a larger internet site).

post   to put information online.

query   a question.

reinforce   to stress; give added strength or support to something.

reputable   trustworthy; having a good reputation; respectable.

revenue   a company's income before costs are taken into account; gross income.

search engine   a computer programme designed to find Internet links that match your search.

Silicon Valley   region in the San Francisco Bay Area of Northern California. It is home to many of the world's largest technology corporations.

Street View   a feature in Google Maps and Google Earth that provides views from various positions along many streets in the world.

waver   to hesitate or be unsure about something.

unique   one of a kind; unequalled.

AdSense   14, 15

AdWords   14, 15

Bezos, Jeff   10

Bing   5, 12, 26

Bock, Laszlo   17

Brin, Sergey   5, 8, 9, 10, 11, 12,15, 18, 24

Cerf, Vinton   27

cookies   6

Excite   7, 12

Gmail   23, 26

Google Earth   5, 22, 25, 26

Google Maps   5, 22, 23, 26

Google News   16, 23, 25

human Resources (HR)   17

Kedar, Ruth   12,13

Kordestani, Omid   21

Lycos   12, 25

Mayer, Marissa   25

MySpace   25

Page, Larry   5, 8, 9, 10, 11, 12,15, 18, 24

PageRankTM   6, 19

Schmidt, Eric   27

Silicon Valley   16

stock market   18

Street View   5, 23, 26

TV networks   21, 22, 24, 25, 28, 29

Unique Selling Proposition (USPs)   7, 29

Stanford University   8, 10, 11

Wojcicki, Susan   23

Yahoo   5, 7, 12, 23, 25, 26

YouTube   5, 12, 20, 21, 25, 26

Google